PUFFIN BOOKS

# A MILLION WAYS
# TO A FAIRER WORLD

This is a very special book. It has been written by children for children, and every copy purchased will go some way to helping children and adults throughout the world to have a better life.

In Oxfam's 50th year, we asked schools in the United Kingdom and overseas to find out how their pupils would ensure a fairer world for others. The response was terrific, showing just how much children care for the earth and all its inhabitants. There are articles, poems, games, puzzles, drawings as well as simple practical statements and ways to help raise awareness of the needs of the world.

Since 1942 Oxfam has been working with poor people around the world, together trying to make a fairer world. Everyone who took part in the *Million Ways to a Fairer World* challenge and sent in contributions to this book is a part of this work. Everyone who reads this book and tries out some of the ideas, or who talks to others about how to make the world a fairer place, is also a part of this working for a fairer world.

Show YOU care. Read this book – it's good, practical and you'll enjoy it too.

All royalties from the sale of this book will go to Oxfam to support its work with poor people, working for a fairer world.

Oxfam

# A Million Ways to a Fairer World

*Cartoons by Angela Martin*

**PUFFIN BOOKS**

The views and facts expressed by the contributors in this book are
not necessarily those held by Oxfam or Puffin Books.
Full names and ages have been credited where information was
available. Apologies to those appearing as anon!

PUFFIN BOOKS

Published by the Penguin Group
Penguin Books Ltd, 27 Wrights Lane, London W8 5TZ, England
Penguin Books USA Inc., 375 Hudson Street, New York, New York 10014, USA
Penguin Books Australia Ltd, Ringwood, Victoria, Australia
Penguin Books Canada Ltd, 10 Alcorn Avenue, Toronto, Ontario, Canada M4V 3B2
Penguin Books (NZ) Ltd, 182–190 Wairau Road, Auckland 10, New Zealand

Penguin Books Ltd, Registered Offices: Harmondsworth, Middlesex, England

Published in Puffin Books 1992
1 3 5 7 9 10 8 6 4 2

Typeset by DatIX International Limited, Bungay, Suffolk
Filmset in Monophoto Plantin
Printed in England by Clays Ltd, St Ives plc

# CONTENTS

# POEM FOR OXFAM

On October 5th 1942,
Some people said: 'What can we do?
There's war in Europe far and near,
Children here and there all fear.
In Greece we know the blockade's on,
How can we help those starving there?'
Then into action Oxfam went,
The Red Cross helped and food was sent,
So started Oxfam's fairer world.

Now fifty years have floated by,
And Oxfam's work just did not die,
Where help was needed they replied . . .
'We'll raise money and send supplies,
And answer all Emergency Appeals –
A better life and fairer deals
For all the poor and refugees,
Our aim to us is very clear
So help we'll send both far and near.'

Now when we hear of wars or storms,
Of unfair trade or selfish ways,
We know that Oxfam's there to aid.
In Oxfam gift shops we can find
Fair-trade goods of every kind,
Toys and games and paper too,
Recycled products and not a few.
And so to Oxfam Gift Shops we all race
To make this world a fairer place.

*2nd Year Pupils*
*Le Verseau International School, Belgium*

# 1

# A FAIRER WORLD

We're working for a fair and kind World.

**F**ood for the starving ones
Protecting **A**nimals
**I**nternational Co-operation
**R**educing trash
**E**ducation for everyone
**R**educe drugs

Keeping the **W**ater clean
Saving **O**zone layer
Maintain **R**ainforests
**L**ove
No more **D**oubt

*Rie Umekawa*
*Yuki Doi*
*Kazuko Hanzawa*
*Reiko Fujii*

*Julia Wheate*

## A Fairer World for Everyone

The shores on which we walk and
The walls in which we talk,
The ground on which we stand,
Both sea and land,
Belongs to all of us,
Those who walk, crawl, scamper or catch the
    no. 11 bus,
We are all equal,
Those who are poor,

Those who are rich,
Those who can't open doors
But have them opened for them,
Those who can't eat,
And those who have seats pulled out for them.
So why are we excluding people
And making them suffer,
When we are all equal?
Why not make it a fairer world
For all of us?

*Hollie Walton*   (*11*)

---

Dear Mr Green MP,

Our planet is precious and should be
looked after. I am worried that when
I grow up the world will be
completely destroyed. Laws should be
made that everyone should look
after the environment to protect
the air we breathe, the water we
drink, the world that we know and
the animals we love.
Green is my favourite colour being
green is a way of life that everyone
should follow.

Yours faithfully
Tom Hooker   (10)

## It Would be a Fairer World if . . .

. . . it rained as much in Africa.

*Suzannah Mellor*   (5)

. . . a basic minimum diet was offered to every human being in the world.

*anon.*

. . . we learned about people in developing countries by watching slides, videos and reading books.

*Melanie Howarth*

## Help

People are starving everywhere,
But other people just don't care.
The water's filthy, the air is dry,
When you go out there you just wanna cry.

More of them are dying every day,
We must try to help them in every way.
The situation is getting worse,
It's like the land is under a curse.
They have no clothes, and nothing to eat.
They don't have shoes to cover their feet.
While lucky children shout and play,
Other people just sit and pray.

*Rachel Veasey     Clare McGarrigle*
*Gemma Burton     Mary Carter*

## How About Underwater

Has it ever occurred to you, have you ever thought how much more sea there is in this world? Well the world is made up of two-thirds sea and one-third land. So if you can find minerals on land, why not try looking for them in the sea? Instead of digging up the land which is small and could be used for more useful things such as villages, animal reserves or plantations, why not dig under the sea which people do not use so much? The sea is vast and much bigger than the land, therefore if you only used a mile of sea, all sea creatures would not lose their homes. Boats could sail over the mine and only a square mile of the sea-bed would be affected.

Oil rigs could also be improved. If there was just a pump at the bottom of the sea, nothing could be destroyed by a hurricane or a rough sea, and no fire could make it history.

How about an underwater village. All you need is a doorway underneath the house, and highly pressurized air to keep water out. Then you are in a normal house with a coral garden, numerous fish and underwater views.

You can have a pet shop that sells dolphins, whales, tiger-sharks and even octopuses.

This could save an awful lot of material, land and lives. Just think how much these ideas could change the world.

*Emma Padmore*   (*10*)

Dear Oxfam,

In the occasion of your 50 years humanitarian help you offered to the world, we wish you all the best!

Go on showing how the world should live together in this difficult life designed by people.

*Krosno Odrzanskie High School*

*Tim Chapman*  (14)

# Why Didn't Anyone Ask Me?

Why didn't anyone ask me,
if I wanted cars to puff smoky fumes
into the fresh air?

Why didn't anyone ask me,
if I wanted to grow up in a world of
fighting countries?

Why didn't anyone ask me,
if I wanted to live in a world where
there's always hazards and dangers?

Why didn't anyone ask me,
if I wanted the countryside to be over-
run by motorways and roads?

Why didn't anyone ask me,
if I wanted different kinds of people,
to fight?

Why didn't anyone ask me,
if I wanted the sea to be filled with
oil.

Why didn't anyone ask me,
if I wanted beautiful and rare animals
to be killed by human greed.

Why didn't anyone ask me,
if I wanted people to be starving,
Maybe it's because it's an unfair world?

*Rosemary J Staves*   *(10)*

## CRACK THE CODE

| | |
|---|---|
| A = 52 | N = 26 |
| B = | O = |
| C = | P = |
| D = | Q = |
| E = | R = |
| F = | S = |
| G = | T = |
| H = | U = |
| I = | V = |
| J = | W = |
| K = | X = |
| L = | Y = |
| M = | Z = 2 |

$$F = 29 + 13 \qquad X = 10 - 4 \qquad R = 360 \div 20$$

When you've cracked the code have a go at working out the words below:

**Clue** – they're all developing countries

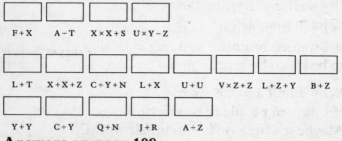

| F + X | A − T | X × X + S | U × Y − Z |
|---|---|---|---|

| L + T | X + X + Z | C ÷ Y + N | L + X | U + U | V × Z + Z | L + Z + Y | B + Z |
|---|---|---|---|---|---|---|---|

| Y + Y | C ÷ Y | Q + N | J + R | A ÷ Z |
|---|---|---|---|---|

**Answers on page 108**

*Kelly-Anne Ransome*

## A Better World

Kids in the west
get all the best
Vaccines to keep healthy
money to be wealthy
But what's left for the rest?

So little to eat
no shoes for their feet
no vaccines or medicine here
leprosy's not a long ago fear
That's what's left for the rest.

We've so much food – it goes bad
The Third World has none – it's so sad
We've got rain – a mixture of weather
They've got summers – lasting for ever
What's to do for the best?

We share our stuff
We've more than enough
Dig deep wells – make water flow
By working together food will grow
That's what's best.

*Vincent Jones.*

## Help Machine

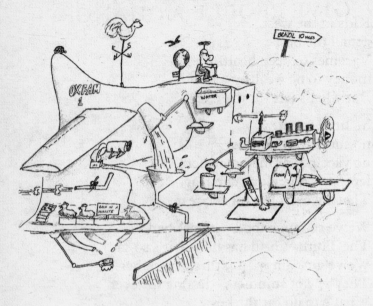

*Tony Parsons* (14)

# 2
# GIVE PEOPLE A CHANCE

## Apartheid

The rioting crowd
Unite, and they're one
All fighting to live free
Under the sun

The bullets rain down
But the crowd still go on
Though some are now missing
Killed by a gun

The people were close,
To freedom, so near
But now they lay resting
In an ocean of tears.

*Kelly Monan*

Black and white people in South Africa should
have the same standard of school, with the same
facilities. If the children want to go to school
together then they should be allowed to decide.

*Adam Morrish*

I think that the world would be a better place
by treating everyone equally and letting everyone
have the same amount of food. They should treat
everyone the same. I think the way some white
people treat black people is terrible. I mean some
white people don't sell homes to black people so
they end up on the streets. Some if they are lucky
end up in a flat in terrible conditions.

*Angela Faulkner*

## They Were There First

When white settlers found the 'New World' i.e.
North America, they claimed it as their own, but
the land already had occupants, the native
Americans known by the white people as Red
Indians. The settlers could not share the land
even though it was not theirs! Hostilities broke
out. The settlers had guns, the Native Americans
had clubs, arrows, bows. Millions of Native
Americans were wiped out. Those who survived
were sent to live on reservations where the land
was poor. How about holding talks and giving
back some sites or all?

THIS WAS NOT, IS NOT FAIR!!

*Amy Ripley*


Stop destroying primitive tribes (like Indians of
the rain forest) by changing their way of life
because they are not 'civilized'.

*Ben Fitzsimmons*   (*10*)


I don't think that it is fair that some African
tribes have had their homes destroyed by other
people just so that they can mine gold and
minerals.

*Marinder Bhogal*   (*10*)

## Namecalling

Why is it unfair on my cousin to be called names?
The names are called out of spite. Some of these
names are 'Nigger', 'Black Jack' and the comment,
'Go back to your own country', which are not
nice and make her upset.

It was difficult for her when her mum and
step-father got married, for she had to move from
town to town as her step-father was moved in his
job.

As she travelled and started each new school,
she would be called names. Now she is twelve she
has learnt to live with these names but they still
hurt her, and she sometimes wishes she was white
instead of black.

But why is it unfair to be called names? If we
weren't called names the world would be a much

nicer place. How would you like it if you had large ears or a wonky nose or you were disabled and kept being called either big ears, funny nose or a spastic? You wouldn't like it, nor does my cousin.

My cousin reacts by calling them names too or telling her mum but that doesn't resolve anything and she is still hurt. When my cousin is called a name and I am with her I react by having a go at them and regretting it afterwards, but I always have to say what I think. When Jemma is called a name I feel as hurt and upset as she is.

My advice to people is that they should never judge a person by their appearance. Get to know them first. Never call people names just for the fun of it. You might be in a car crash yourself and end up in a wheelchair and then get called names yourself, just because you are different.

So think before you open your mouth.

*Louise Hathaway*   *(12)*

## Does it Matter?

Why does the colour of your skin
Dictate the life you're involved in.
It's just your envelope
It's not a sin
Just concentrate on what's within.

*Kelly Monan*   *(14)*

I think people should judge their friends by their personality not by their skin or how fat they are or whatever.

*Mark Gilchrist*

All people are equal according to many religious and political beliefs. Unfortunately this isn't the case in many societies, where people are judged by the colour of their skin or by their religious beliefs, or by their social class. But nobody chooses where they are born, or to whom. Children should be taught at school to realize that everyone is truly equal. Being different does not mean being unequal.

*Claudia Briones   (12)*

In South America sewer children are not loved. Sewer children are hated by the police. It's not fair.

*Matthew Ol*

## Looks Aren't Everything

It all started when I moved to Detroit, Michigan (USA).

I did not want to move as I had all my friends back in England, but that was a different matter to my parents.

It took me a couple of weeks to settle in, but I

was so miserable as the only kid on my street was a spastic boy who used to run around the street like a baby in its diaper. Every time I saw the spastic boy I used to look away quickly and call him names underneath my breath. I hated the sight of him.

We had been living in the USA for over a year and I started to pick up the accent. I had not seen the spastic boy for over a week, but I wasn't really bothered as most of the time I was with my friends . . . But there was one problem, I wasn't pleased as Mum and Dad had made some new friends: some friends who happened to be the one and only spastic boy's mum and dad.

Mum knew that I disliked the spastic boy, but she always said to me, 'Looks aren't everything.' I used to pretend to ignore her and start singing.

It was late at night, when we heard a load of shouting across the road. I put my head around the curtain and took a good look around outside and there before my eyes I saw a load of kids from the eleventh grade teasing and throwing stones at the spastic boy. All of a sudden I felt pity for the spastic boy and I felt as if I was in his position. Then with a sorrowful look the spastic kid looked at me. My heart sank to the bottom of my feet, I felt so guilty.

So for the next few weeks I thought about what happened on that night and always regretted that I never did anything to help him.

*Kelly Squires*

## Care for the Old Folk . . .

We would like to think that when we are watching
television in front of the fire, that old people are
doing the same. It would be fair to make sure that
enough money is raised to keep them comfortable.
Hospitals should get more money so that they can
pay more people to care for OAPs. It would be
fair to see that they are well looked after.

*Leanne Melvin*
*Gavin Petrie*

It's not fair that old people can't work, because
some old people can, and they look weak but
some aren't. If I ruled the world I would let them
work if they wanted to and if they were strong

enough. I would make them gardens and put posters up for jobs for old people. I would make more old people's homes and get someone to come round to do exercises with them and give them electric wheel chairs and put up the pension.

I think we should build more leisure centres near houses for old people, and by schools. Not huge, not too small, but large enough. If the leisure centre was not far away, the elderly people could walk, or ride instead of taking a mini bus. Schools might have to take a coach, but it is not that far. It would mean that children are getting more exercise, and old people are getting out and having fun. The building may take time, and money, and it may be difficult, but in the long run it will be worth it.

*Kimberly Jenkins*

## ... and the Disabled ...

It is not fair because some people are deaf or blind and some people can't walk. These people are called disabled. The people who are blind sometimes have guide dogs. The people who can't walk have wheelchairs. If I was in charge I would put ramps for the people who can't walk. I would give the people that can't walk electric wheelchairs. I would give the people who are deaf hearing aids. People in shops should know sign language.

## . . . and Look After Your Health

**DO NOT SMOKE CIGARETTES** because it is bad for your life. It's bad to smoke cigarettes in the petrol station because it could explode the petrol station. Smoking is a bad habit, it may cause dangerous diseases affecting the lungs and heart. Smoking causes many fires in houses and factories and companies and in different places.

*Ahmed E*   (9)

## Drugs

We should say 'NO' to drugs because it has taken the lives of many people. And if people would stop selling drugs to people and start selling medicine instead it would stop people from dying. We must not take drugs in any way.

*Akbar*   (9)

## Homelessness

The Homeless are starving, the Homeless are weak, with nowhere to stay, with nowhere to sleep.
The Homeless live in a cardboard box without any doors, without any locks, outside the box the wind is howling,

among the streets people are prowling.
The Homeless beg outside the shops
and sometimes get picked up by the cops.
To make some money they need an education
which makes them forced into prostitution.
We can help them if we try.
But if we don't then some will Die.

*anon*

All the millionaires could donate money to appeals
for the homeless, starving children and people in
Africa.

*Polly Sturgess*

When I watch the television it makes me feel sad
when I see homeless people. They have to sleep
outside in the cold and rain, and only have a few
belongings. It is because of their government that
they have no homes and I think it is very unfair.
We could miss our snack and the cost of the
snack could go to the homeless people.

*Charlotte Foster*

I don't think it's fair how some people have to live on the streets and I think we should try to get the government to build a block of flats for them on waste ground.

*Renata Shieff   (11)*

Build more hostels for the homeless.

*Clare Bentley*

## Fairer for the Girls

We are a group of twelve- and thirteen-year-old girls and we are depressed because we cannot do practical work in Art or Music because the boys are so immature and stupid. We will never get a chance to do practical work for a long time.

*Katherine Cordone*

In some countries the men don't let the women do a lot of things like vote. The woman in England were only allowed to vote in approximately 1921 (actually a limited franchise in 1918, with full equal voting rights in 1928 in the UK) but the women in some countries were only allowed to vote very recently. What I think is very fair is that the men should let women have an opinion and therefore have the vote.

*Rosie Micklewright   (11)*

Women should be treated EQUALLY!!!
We don't want to be treated as second class
men!!!

*Jane Nicholls*  *(15)*
*Kirstin Birch*  *(14)*
*Maria Helgstrand*  *(15)*

# 3

# CHILDREN MATTER

## A Children's Charter

1  All Children have a right to be loved.
2  All Children have a right to deal with their own money.
3  All Children have a right to be treated equally.
4  All Children have a right to education.
5  All Children have a right to freedom.
6  All Children have a right to food and drink.
7  All Children have a right to respect.
8  All Children have a right to have more privileges as they get older.
9  All Children have a right to shelter.
10  All Children have a right to decide where they live.

*Class 7V, Attleborough High School, Norfolk*

## On the Outside Looking In

I'm on the outside looking in,
and I'm feeling very lonely.

I wish I had a friend to talk to,
so breaktimes wouldn't pass so slowly.

To join in some games would be nice,
To run about and play,
With all the others having fun,
Maybe I will one day.

Tomorrow I'll try very hard,
To make some friend in class.
Then I can join in with the fun,
The chatter and the laughs.

*Siân Hayes*


## Schooldays

Schooldays are supposed to be the happiest days
of your life. For some children they are the worst
because some children think they haven't got any
friends. Other children get bullied. If you see
someone being bullied tell a teacher so that they
can stop it. Another way is to get your friends
together and go and challenge the bully. Tell the
bully to stop it. Then you could ask the person
who is being bullied to join your group of friends.

## A Friendship Game

This is a good game for playtime.

### HOW TO PLAY

Someone has to be the caller. The caller gets the
children to turn around until he or she shouts
'STOP'. When everyone has stopped they have to
shake hands with the person nearest to them.
Then they have to find out as much as they can
about that person until the caller shouts 'GO'
again. Take it in turns to be the caller and play
until the bell rings!

*Amina Patel*  (10)

FRIENDSHIP GAME

## It Would be Fairer if . . .

. . . we could share our sweets with each other.

*Anja Gibbs* (5)

. . . you share your things with other people because they may not be as lucky as you are.

*Duncan Strain* (7)

. . . we share food with people.

*Elise Williams* (5)

. . . we stop being selfish.

*Jennifer Bone* (5)

. . . you stop teasing children who are not as lucky as you are.

*Antonia Earp* (8)

. . . playgrounds were safer for children so that if they fall they won't hurt themselves.

*Katie Jackson*

. . . there were more playgrounds for children who live on busy roads.

*Christian Catlow*

. . . children of a sensible age had a bit more to
say in divorce. They would not stop the divorce
or anything, but have a little more say in which
parent they saw most. Also I think if a parent
decided to marry again, it would be better if they
could say freely whether or not they liked the
man or lady and be allowed to say whether or not
they still want to see that parent a lot. I think this
might take away some of the misery of a divorce.
I also think people should be encouraged not to
get a divorce, but stay together for as long as
possible and see if things work out.

*Fiona M Dewar*


## I Think . . .

. . . sharing is best.
   Share and make friends or be selfish and lose
friends. If you like making friends then
SHARING is the thing to do.

*anon.*


. . . people should stop bullying and get on with their
OWN lives. They should think about others
more.
PLEASE STOP BULLYING.

*Paula Grant   (10)*

. . . cheating is a horrible thing to do.
People get angry when it is done to them and it
can be called fraud. When you cheat, you cheat
yourself and lose your friends. CHEATING
DOES NOT PAY. DON'T DO IT.

*anon.*

When I watched Anneka Rice on the TV I was
almost crying. Because when I thought how lucky
I am to have a caring mum and dad, a warm
home and food and lots of other things. Those
poor children didn't have anything like that. I
think more people should give clothes, toys and
other things to Oxfam.

*Sarah Jordan*  (9)

I think every child should learn to read because
he or she would get a better education and could
tell the difference between good and evil. Sending
books to other countries so that the people can

read there would help. They do not have books in some countries of Africa and other poor parts of the world. I would like to go to such a place when I am older to help poor and young children learn to read. I hope I can help to make the world a fairer place.

*Rebecca Leslie*

It's not fair that I get blamed for everything my sister does – just because I'm older. Why do adults say things like 'You're the oldest. You should know better!'

*anon.*

# 4

# BE KIND TO ANIMALS

I think the slaughter of horses is bad, as they give us so much joy. They travel over long distances in cramped stalls with no food or bedding. When they have been transported to a foreign country they are put in pens. The pens are small and are very cramped with SIX or SEVEN to a pen. The lucky ones are sold to people who will love them. Then unlucky ones are sold to a butcher who will make meat out of them.

THEY SHOULD BE SAVED.

*Rosey Buckley*

## The Seal

I am a seal
Trapped in a black wave
It is like a cage
It traps anything in its way
When it's got you trapped
It tries to kill you, sometimes it does
Though I got free I nearly died
It was like a nightmare.

*Emma Gardner*   (*11*)

## It's Not Fair on Animals!

If everyone only bought dolphin-friendly tuna,
dolphins would be able to swim about without
the thought that they could get caught in a net
any second.

We should *never* buy make-up tested on animals
and I think it is unfair how they get dogs and
monkeys to test equipment.

Don't eat meat if it comes from the rain forest,
ask the person serving you where the meat comes
from. Try not to eat meat at all as it is unfair for
the animals.

*Tom Hooker*   (*10*)

## I Think . . .

. . . they should stop pheasant shoots because just because they are rich they think that they can kill wildlife.

*James Davies*   (8)

. . . they should stop building on fields which house wildlife and other animals. Save some green places for our children.

*Joanne Kyte*

## The Ivory Hunt

The wildlife is awakening,
The trees begin to sway,
The hunters get their rifles ready
The elephants begin their day.

The hunters click their triggers,
The elephants run for cover,
Baby calves get left behind,
Crying for their mother.

The elephants start to shiver,
Sending fear so sharp,
As hunters come, they scatter,
But one gets hit through the heart.

The elephant falls to the ground,
He makes a tremendous crash,
The hunters creep towards it,
And kick at it like trash.

So at the end of the hunt
With ivory, they go back home
The elephant pulled behind
Dead and all alone.

*Lesley Keer*

## What Ivory is Used for

In certain countries on the earth, some people
still hunt for ivory. Most people hunt for ivory
for jewellery and ornaments. In Africa they hunt
ivory for knife handles. They are making profits at
the expense of the endangered elephants. If there
is such a demand or need for elephants' tusks
why don't they shoot it with a tranquillizer dart
and when it falls asleep just cut the tusks off
instead of killing it. Elephants, in a few years
time, may be extinct if we don't stop ivory
poachers now. So please help the elephants and
please help the world.

*Lesley Keer*

## The Killing

Walking along sleek and cunning,
the coyote stalks the silent forest.
Intrepid, hungry, looking for food,
loyal to his followers.
But his ears come up,
he hears the sound of silent death.
The footsteps of hell,
he turns to run.
But in doing so he receives an extremely hard
    blow.
He falls to the ground thinking
This is it, This is it.
And he is oh so unfortunately right,
one foot upon his neck,
the other upon his chest.
All the coyote can now think of is
DEATH!
He was so innocent,
brave and loyal,
until the life was taken away.
No more would he see the bright blue sky.
No longer would he see the lush green grass.
All of this taken away,
just so people can have some fun.

*Kirstie Cheeseman*

## Whales

Whales are kind.
Whales are friendly.
We are killing them but why.
They don't kill us.
In a few years they will be gone.
We're making it fair for the world,
So why not make it fair for them.

*Nicola Green*

## Unfair to Sloths

Sloths hold on upside down. They have no trees.
A sloth cannot hold upside down if he hasn't got
a tree.

*Chris*

## What I Would do

First of all I would ban all fox, stag and other
hunting as I have heard that it is not a very nice
way to kill animals. I would also ban anyone
trying to capture hedgehogs, foxes or any other
animal by nailing them to a tree and things like
that.

*Thomas Jewell*   *(11)*

## It's Not Fair

I think that killing for fun is unkind and unfair
like hunting whales and foxes. If you were a fox
and a pack of hounds were chasing you what can
you do? Run and hide. Can't there be more
protests and I will keep on writing to the
government until they do something useful for
once.

*Robyn Shelford-Clarke*  (*10*)

It's not fair because animals get killed by
chemicals to see if products will be all right for
us. So if we bought things from shops that don't
have things that are tested on animals, animals
will not be treated so badly.

*Charlotte Burton*  (*10*)

IT'S NOT FAIR IT'S NOT FAIR IT'S NOT FAIR IT'S NOT FAIR

THE WORLD WOULD BE A FAIRER
PLACE IF ANIMALS WERE NOT
KILLED FOR THEIR FUR

How would YOU like to be stripped
of your fur coat in the cold?

IT'S NOT FAIR IT'S NOT FAIR IT'S NOT FAIR IT'S NOT FAIR

*Vicki*

Every time we cut down trees, make new roads or
dig up the hedges around the fields, we destroy
an animal's home. If we are not careful animals
will be extinct. Famine, drought, disease and
floods also kill animals. With all these forces
working together some species are already extinct,
for example the Tasmanian Wolf and the
Passenger Pigeon.

Many monkeys are endangered as the tropical
rain forests are being cut down to clear land for
farming and building. The tropical rain forests
are not only beautiful but they provide shelter for
orchids and some rare plants of the pineapple
family and help keep the world's climate and
atmosphere stable.

*Kate Miller*

Animals don't smoke
Animals don't pollute
Animals don't war
So why do they suffer?

*anon.*

# 5

# CARE FOR THE ENVIRONMENT

This could be such a beautiful world if the seas
  and rivers and streams were clean and sparkling.
Don't throw your rubbish into the streams.
Don't pollute the seas.
Don't ruin your rivers.

This could be such a beautiful world if all the
  skies were blue and clean.
Don't pollute your air.
Don't use CFCs.
Don't use leaded petrol.

This could be such a beautiful world if all our
    streets were clean once again.
Don't throw down litter.
Use a bin.

This could be such a beautiful world if all the
    animals could play without being afraid.
Don't shout for fun.
Next time, think before you act.
Take care of your countryside.
Take care of your world.

*Rebecca Gates*   *(11)*

## Pollution isn't the Solution

To make the world fairer it would be better if the
environment was better. Just because your hair
doesn't do what you want it to do you have to use
hairspray, but you could always use water or hair
gel. Because of this, the hole in the ozone layer
gets a little bigger each time. If the ozone layer
disappears we will no longer be protected from
the ultraviolet rays of the sun and therefore our
skin will burn. Also pollution is an enemy to our
environment. There have been so many oil
spillages that the fish in the rivers, seas and oceans
are dying. Pollution is also caused by cars. The
solution to this problem would be if more people
ride bikes. In this way it would reduce the
pollution. If the government introduced cycle

lanes around the country, more people would be
encouraged to ride their bikes. The adults have
the power, but the children do not and therefore
the adults can use their power to make the
environment a better place to live in. So
remember the world's best friend is you.

*Shahela Islam*

We could make a better world if people used
solar power or wind power. If factories could put
a dome on the chimney, the dome could collect
all the poisonous gases. They they could send it
up into space and then they could blow it up. It
would help stop air pollution.

*Paul Adams*

Pollution is like a drug which keeps being fed into the world but if we try we can stop this killer and save our world.

There are hundreds of types of pollution around the world which do their bit of eating away at our health and the ozone layer. You might start wondering why pollution might affect your health. Well, we all know that car exhausts have a disgusting smell. Babies and toddlers are at the height of exhaust pipes so the fumes are breathed in.

People don't understand that the more we drop rubbish the more the world suffers. Picture a beautiful countryside which has had a family camping there. Imagine that there are crisp packets and other bits of rubbish scattered around. Not only would the view be spoiled but animals can suffocate on rubbish and also these things are not biodegradeable.

So please take care of our world for our children and our children's children, so they can enjoy it too!

*Sharan G*
*Rachael Mc*


## It's Not Fair

It's not fair that we are doing lots of horrible things to the environment. We should stop doing things to the environment and change our ways so that we can breathe in cleaner air and see a better world. We can do a lot of things to help the world and the creatures in it. For example we could start eating tuna that is dolphin-friendly and send letters to an MP asking him if he could try and get other MPs to help to stop factories dumping toxic waste into streams, rivers and seas. We should also help to try and stop trees being cut down by again asking an MP to try and get other MPs on your side.

*Catherine Edwards*  (*10*)

To My MP
Any town
Great Britain
WOR LD I

59 Ickleford Rd
Hitchin
Herts Sg5 1TS

Dear M.P.
    I feel extremely upset that all the rainforests are being cut down just so farmers can breed animals then kill them. Who needs meat anyway? If we eat plenty of things with protein in, save meat, we would all be very healthy.

    Yours faithfully
    Gillian Eva

Age 10

## Environmental Wordsearch

```
R O S N O I T A V R A T S Q
R G Z P I T S U A H X E W U
P R B O V B T S M O K E P E
U E O L N T E C K J R W N I
N E T L W E L B A A A B E F
E N T U R H L V K C I L S U
N H L T C S A A T M N U A M
I O E I G A D L Y V F R E E
A U B O T D R F E E O H S S
R S A N G T F S Q S R A I S
D E N X T C N I T X E P D S
I G K H O M E L E S S T D E
C H W A S T E F I N T D A X
A T A Y E Y W D B B O L I O
```

| | |
|---|---|
| ACID RAIN | OZONE-LAYER |
| BOTTLEBANK | POLLUTION |
| CARS | RAIN FOREST |
| DISEASE | SLICK |
| EXHAUST | SMOKE |
| EXTINCT | STARVATION |
| FUMES | TREES |
| GREENHOUSE | WASTE |
| HOMELESS | WHALES |
| OIL | |

**Answers on page 108**

To make a fairer world I think they should ban all CFCs because they destroy the ozone layer. Every year the length of a football pitch of the ozone layer is destroyed. If it is destroyed all the sun's rays will eventually get through and slowly melt the ice in the polar regions and the water level will gradually rise and cause terrible floods. CFC (Chlorofluorocarbon) is a man-made gas used in airconditioning, fridges etc. The gases released from this product collect in the upper atmosphere and form chlorine monoxide which destroys the ozone layer.

*Sharear Farid*

I think what would make a fairer world would be if people stopped cutting down the rain forests, because they are very important to both man and animals. The animals need the rain forests for their homes, and humans need them because there is a lot of helpful medicine which could save people's lives. Rain forests also affect the climate and if all the trees disappeared it might change the balance of the weather completely. The more trees cut down, the more plants die, and plants produce oxygen which will help us breathe more easily.

*Kirstin Inglefield*

I have eczema and in a way it is good because I can't use aerosols. If someone smokes it pollutes your world and you and your pocket. STOP polluting the world so the next generation can live their life happily too.

*anon.*

## On Your Bike!

At the moment there is a lot about the greenhouse effect in everybody's minds. Part of the problem is ours. We don't usually think, but the food we eat comes in lorries and leaves in lorries. From the lorries exhausts come fumes of carbon dioxide and nitrous oxide, which build up in the air creating the greenhouse effect. If we could find a new way of transport it might cut down on exhaust fumes. Instead of driving to work in a car, how about riding to work on a bike or walking?

*Elizabeth Wheeler*

Have you ever noticed that some cities are filled with smoke? Traffic fumes are the problem. All these cars roaming around the streets, their exhaust pipes leaving smoke behind. This should not be happening! We don't want smoky towns – people choking to death! My idea is that more people should have cars that run on unleaded petrol. Also if you are travelling a short distance, go by bike. Bike rides are fun too and very good for you.

*Nicola Fleming*

I think there should be no cars on the road, as cars pollute the world. It is healthier if people walk or cycle. This could stop a lot of wars because people wouldn't have to fight over the oil. Also not so many people would have lost their lives. I chose to write about this because it is unfair on people who either give their lives for something that anybody could prevent happening or that use unleaded petrol to save our world when all others do is endanger it by using leaded petrol.

*anon.*

*Amy Badcock*

*Madeleine Ding*   (9)

## Pick up Your Litter!

Littering the towns ain't very nice.
That would attract loads of mice.
If we make a stop to all our litter,
The towns would look a great deal better.
To stop putting litter on the ground
There should be more bins around.
We must make the effort,
To put rubbish in the bins,
AND THAT'S OUR METHOD!

*anon.*

I think there should be stricter rules for people
walking through farms. Walkers keep dropping
litter on the ground. They must think the farmers
are going to pick it up for them. They should
keep their dogs on leads because they chase our
sheep. There are people trying to build a walkway
through our farm at the moment, but our dad
says it would not be fair to the animals.

*David Watson and Adam Smith*

## Trees are Triff!

- Did you know that trees help us breathe? They
  make oxygen from the gas we breathe out.
- Trees keep the air clean.
- Trees bring rain as they keep the air damp.
- They give us food like nuts and plants give us
  vegetables and tea and coffee.
- They give animals and insects homes.

SO TREAT THEM WITH RESPECT.
PLANT A TREE IN YOUR GARDEN.

*Ben Jones*   *(12)*

If we buy wooden items: toys, pencil-boxes, we should make sure they are not made of tropical hardwood. The rain forests should be saved. Find out what wood wooden toys are made of and if you don't know then don't buy.

*anon.*

## Look After our Neighbourhood

I think that some villages in our area need a few speed limits and a lot of street lights, because of the cars which go at 70 mph round a dangerous bend and sometimes cause accidents.

We need street lights to help people who walk home in the dark, to see the street ahead. Some villages haven't even got any street lights.

My solution is that the county council could install a few street lights and help get lower speed limits in some villages.

I think for a fairer world we should stop letting dogs foul parklands because it spoils nature and spreads germs.

We could improve the world by looking after the churchyard. Look after the other places as well as the parks and that.

My idea for a fairer world is that everybody

should be kinder to the environment because if everybody keeps throwing things on the floor imagine what the world will be like in about six years time. Although there are road-sweepers and dustmen, they can't get under hedges. Our world would be fairer then because it would not be horrible, it would be nicer.

*Kate Walker*

Make most cars electric, similar to milk vans. It would help keep the pollution down by about 75%. Trams could be used as buses. The government would have to work out where the tram tracks go to and would have to subsidize the cost of using the trams and electric cars so everybody could afford to use them.

*Richard G*  (*10*)

## The Wider World

This world was clean when it was new but now it is a terrible view, try to help!

*anon.*

Have you ever seen a picture taken by an astronaut? What have you felt? I felt that it's beautiful. Its blueness freshened up my feelings.

But if you look at it closer, on this planet there
are lots of things happening now. But we don't
care. That's the problem: we couldn't be bothered
to save the Earth.
So, Love for Earth.
Earth for us.
Peace.

*Hyon-Jung Chang*   *(14)*

Do not let your camels eat all the ghraf trees
otherwise the desert will be all sand.

*Erland*   *(7)*

# 6

# SAVE OUR RESOURCES

Only take what you really need. We all use too much electricity, too much metal, too many trees and too much oil. If we use less of everything and recycle things there will be more for future generations. So:

- Pick up cans, expecially aluminium ones as these can help make bicycles, saucepans and even bits of aeroplanes.
- Take the cans to a recycling centre, but clean them first.
- Save electricity – turn lights off
   – ask your parents to buy energy-saving light bulbs
   – wear warmer clothes instead of turning the heat up

- Don't waste trees! – reuse old birthday cards
  – use both sides of paper
  – don't have carrier bags from the shops

- Keep a box for old comics and newspapers. Take them to a recycling centre. Ask your friends to help.

- Take clothes and toys you don't want but that other people may want to an Oxfam shop.

Remember – what you don't want someone else might!
Recycle it! Waste not, want not!

*Siân Edwards*  (12)

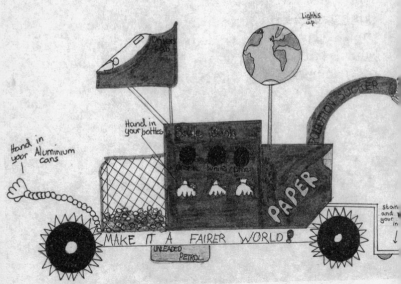

*Matthew Burns and Paul MacKie*  (10)

## I Warned Them

Why did the humans take no heed?
I warned them to watch their greed.
They covered the sea with sludgy oil
and mixed toxic waste in with the soil.
They polluted their rivers,
they stripped the land
there's nothing left
but dust and sand.
I warned them when the world was new
about the awful things
that they could do,
but they did not listen,
they did not care,
now all I can do
is stand and stare.

*Eleni Bide*   *(11)*

**Which Line?**

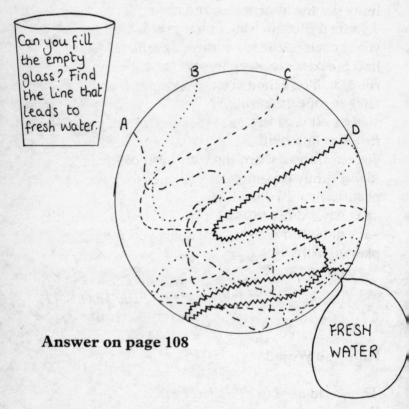

Can you fill the empty glass? Find the line that leads to fresh water.

FRESH WATER

**Answer on page 108**

**'Waste Not, Want Not.'**

My mother is always saying those words. So before you throw anything away, stop and think. Could someone else use it?

Charities like Oxfam and Guide Dogs for the Blind are often pleased to have old stamps, milk bottle tops, toys, books and clothes. Never throw

away plastic bags – use them again and again.
When they get really tatty you can use them to
line your waste-paper basket.

Take egg boxes back to local shops and reuse
your envelopes. Have you got a garden? If you
have, make a compost heap to recycle vegetable
rubbish. You can then use the compost as a
fertilizer for the garden.

Take all your bottles, cans, papers and rags to
the recycling centre. If you don't know where
your nearest is, then ring your local council.

Don't buy paper napkins or cups for your
parties – it's a waste of paper.

YOU CAN HAVE FUN WITHOUT WASTE
– it's more fun because you know you're helping
planet Earth!

*Wayne Thomas   (12)*

## Help the World

The world used to be a lovely place
But that was before the human race
We've ravaged it and savaged it,
and looted it and polluted it;
Now we must start a new operation
and help along the new generation,
Giving pride back to our earth
returning it to its proper worth.

*Mark Toynbee   (9)*

## Crossword for a Fairer World

CLUES

### Across

1. Harmful gases found in aerosol sprays. (4)
4. If you can use it again, you don't need to waste it you can . . . (7)
6. If you buy this type of tuna you are helping these mammals that swim in the sea. (7/8)
8. Looking after the natural world around us – a word we should all know. (12)
9. A wooded tropical area which is often very wet. (4/6)
11. Contamination of the environment. (9)
12. If your can of hairspray or furniture polish has one of these you could be damaging the ozone layer. (7)
14. If you use this type of petrol, you are reducing pollution. (8)
15. No matter what colour you are, if you are concerned about environment you are definitely . . . (5)

### Down

1. This cause of lead pollution is seen a lot in road traffic. (3/5)
2. This colourful organization is dedicated to conservation. (10)
3. This type of rain is caused by water pollution and is killing our trees. (4)
5. If we don't protect our wildlife we will . . . their lives. (8)
7. A word to describe your surroundings. (11)
10. Although we can't see this, it is all the air surrounding the earth. (10)
13. What tiny animals can get trapped in, so always put them in the bin. (4)

**\* Special Clue**

An organization that helps poor people around the world. (5)

**Answers on page 109**

*Katherine Devereux* (10)

## Recycle it!

Recycle bottles. Make sure that rubbish goes in bins, and tell your mum and dad to use lead-free petrol.

*J R Quinn*

Recycling is the best thing we can do. I especially like to go down to the bottle bank and plop the bottle into the bank and hear the clatter.

*Laura Morley*

## Learn About the Environment

The more you know about the problems, the more you will be able to do to help solve them. Read the newspapers – especially the ones for 'Young People'. There are 'green' magazines too and *Blue Peter* always has features, so watching TV can help too!

Perhaps you have a 'wild patch' in your town where you can learn about wildlife. We have one called Camley Street – it's near King's Cross – we hope it doesn't close down. We've written letters to our local council to help save it. Is there something you need to write to your local council or MP for? It's important for children to make their voices heard.

You can join groups to help the environment like Greenpeace or the Friends of the Earth.

So don't just sit there – do something!

*Lorna Masters*   *(10)*

The government should set up more recycling depots. Thousands of tonnes of waste is dumped every month in England. All this waste gives off methane gas which is harmful to the atmosphere. If we had more recycling centres that would be fairer for future generations.

*anon.*

## The Stratosphere Airship

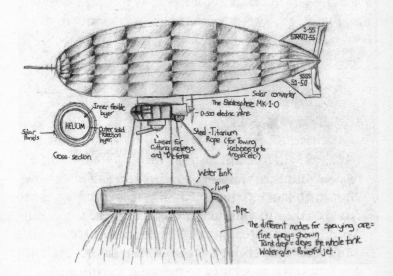

*Joe Morris*   *(14)*

## Use What we Have Used!

I think we should use recycled paper, it's a
catastrophe that we never use it in school. Here's
what I think – we should use what we've used.

*Philip Linfield*

If there was an easier way to recycle plastic, cans,
foil, bottle tops etc maybe more people would do
it. People should get a different-coloured garbage
bag to put the cans etc they want to recycle in.
Also if programmes (like *Blue Peter*) raise money
by collecting aluminium cans, they should sell
people yellow, or light-purple garbage bags. That
way people would not have to drive to, say
Safeways, which (for some people like me) can be
a long drive. This process will not cost much
money, so why is it not done?

*Kimberley Jenkins*

## Riddle-me-Rees

My first is in bus but not in car
My second is in train but not in far
My third is in city but it's not in town
My fourth is in yellow but not in brown
My fifth is in care, and also in clean
My sixth is in eleven but not in thirteen
My whole's a good way to travel, it's clean and
green!

My first is in wet but not in dry
My second's in ouch but not in cry
My third is in run but not in walk
My fourth is in Ludlow but not in Cork
My fifth is in Dublin but not in Eire
My whole is a place that needs to be fairer.

*Alison Clarke*  (8)

**Answers on page 109**

# 7

# WAR, POVERTY AND STRIFE

## War, Poverty and Strife

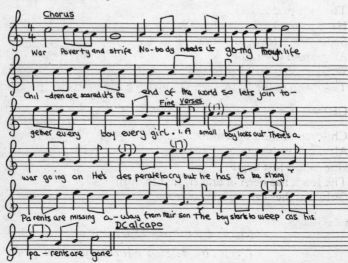

CHORUS:
> *War, Poverty and Strife*
> *Nobody needs it going through life*
> *Children are scared it's the end of the world*
> *So let's join together every boy every girl*

A small boy looks out
There's a war going on
He's desperate to cry
But he has to be strong
Parents are missing away from their son
The boy starts to weep 'cause his parents are gone

CHORUS

A small girl looks weak
Her bones start to show
She needs to eat
But to work she must go
Her brother is ill and destined to die
She looks up to heaven there's no hope in the sky.

CHORUS

The kids in the class
Have no books at school
Soon they'll leave for work
At thirteen it's a rule
What's going on what future's in store
They'll go to the factories no money for any more.

CHORUS

Children of the world unite as one
Although we've almost finished
Our song's just begun
The torch has been lit and started to burn
Only together can we start to learn

CHORUS

*Music by Claire Dyer*
*Lyrics by Jessica Moriarty*    *(both 14)*

## Poverty in the Slums

Walking through those desolate streets,
Many people you will meet,
They will tell you of their life,
Of disease and death running rife.

The source of life is not far away,
It runs through the night, and day after day.
These people must use their source of breath,
But, that only lifeline frequently becomes death.

Excrement makes the drinking water worse,
Drinking this adds to the curse.
Boil the water and you may be saved,
Then, a street to recovery may be paved.

Before the problem reduces its ferocity,
The makeshift homes must be supplied with
  electricity.
This could take many more years,
And will only add to the veil of tears.

But, why should people live in the slums,
And live on barely more than crumbs?
Not half a mile from absolute poverty,
Are towering buildings, relishing in their novelty.

If work is found by someone in a slum,
His wages are of the lowest sum.
He cannot refuse this slave labour,
This work he has always to savour.

Fresh water and jobs of sufficient pay,
Will give these people a better say.
Then maybe, one day, near and fair,
Will make this world know and care.

*Justin Ventham*  *(14)*

## War Unfair

War is cruel and people cry,
And I think the army
    should know why they
Raid houses and leave people to die.

*Craig Jones   (11)*

No fighting on any day that has a 'y' in it =
PEACE.

*anon.*

When two countries disagree on something
instead of war they could meet together and
discuss it.

*Hannah Brook*

There are many kinds of disputes going on in the
world today. There are the two children in school
arguing about who is going to be first in the queue.
There is the married couple arguing about whose
turn it is to change the baby's nappy at night.
There is the divorced couple arguing about who
has access to their children. Then there are two
countries arguing and fighting about leadership –
but on a larger scale, with real weapons.

However small or large these arguments may
be, without them the world would be a happier
and more peaceful place.

*Alexandra Craigen   (12)*

To make the world fairer seems quite impossible, but there are many things that we can do.

The first step is to think before you act – everything else will then follow . . .

*Yoko Nagami* (13)

You need to divide food and money more equally so no one goes hungry while someone else has too much to eat. More money should be diverted into alternative energies instead of things that produce pollution like burning coal or wood, or ones that are really dangerous like nuclear power. There should be restrictions on alcohol and drugs which eventually kill people. Drug-dealers who push children or teenagers into taking drugs or selling them are committing a very grave crime. And there should be no racism. People should be equal whether they are black or white.

*Cecilia Mortimore* (12)

## WORDS TO FIND

SANITATION
RICH
MEDICATION

TRANSPORTATION
GOOD EDUCATION
JOBS

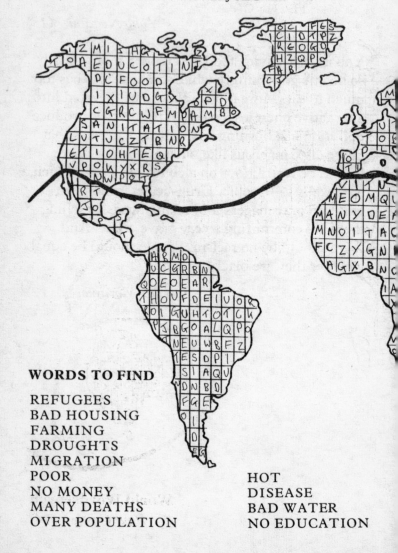

## WORDS TO FIND

REFUGEES
BAD HOUSING
FARMING
DROUGHTS
MIGRATION
POOR
NO MONEY
MANY DEATHS
OVER POPULATION

HOT
DISEASE
BAD WATER
NO EDUCATION

CLEANER          FOOD
LONGER LIFE      CROPS
GOOD WATER       WEALTH
TECHNOLOGY

**World Wordsearch**
*Paul Castle*   *(14)*

# 8

# ACTION FOR A FAIRER WORLD

Put on a play and ask your friends, family and
school to come and see it. The play could be
about something your community needs like:
a zebra crossing outside the play centre,
a swimming-pool just for old people so they don't
get splashed by children.

Buy your Christmas and birthday presents at a
charity shop, like an Oxfam shop, or at a craft
centre that sells goods made in the Third World.
You'll get nice, unusual presents and your money
will go to a good cause.

*anon.*

We take it in turns to visit the old people's home in Alford (our nearest village). They say we cheer them up and they look forward to Wednesday afternoons. I think we are making the world a little bit fairer for them.

*Zoe Hezzell*

## What I Will Do . . .

. . . I will only buy deodorants that are ozone-friendly.

. . . I will stop bullying people.

. . . When we move house I will plant a tree.

. . . I will only eat dolphin-friendly fish.

. . . I will write to an MP about the rain forests being cut down.

. . . I will tell my sister to buy cosmetics that have not been tested on animals.

... I'm going to tell my mum to change her petrol from four star to unleaded.

... I'm going to give my old clothes to Oxfam so they can sell them and use the money to help poor people.

*Pavamdeesch Achal* (*10*)

We formed a Green Team and worked to rescue a lake at the side of the school and cleaned up the area, planted wild flowers and Silver Birch trees, painted up the garden seat, put nesting-boxes in the trees and cleared up our culvert. We got an award from the Council for this – if others did the same our world would certainly look a lot fairer.

*Zoe Ayres* (*10*)

For a better world you could do things like going along to your granny's house and maybe get coal and start a fire for her, or clean out the oven. Or you could go to other people in your neighbourhood that are alone and perhaps do some jobs for them and talk to them and make them feel happy and wanted.

*Mark Barry*

We have renovated a room in the Coach House at school. I have lent my microscope and we are using this room to plan ideas and observe wildlife, keep records, etc. This will make a small part of the world (Well Vale, Lincs) into a fairer place.

*Tom Latham* (*10*)

# A DIFFERENCE IN THE WORLD

Oxfam's reporters Nicki and Sophie have been busy researching about a fairer world. At one point in your life you must have dropped some rubbish even if it is as small as a sweet wrapper or as big as a plastic bag.

Animals can get killed, the land could be destroyed and one day we humans might die out because of breathing in too much polluted air.

Our school had a Bring and Buy sale to raise money for Oxfam's fairer world campaign. We had six stalls: gifts, books and comics, toys, sweets, goodies to eat, and three raffles. Each class was responsible for a stall.

Instead of wearing red noses like on comic relief day we brought in masks. Oxfam reporter Sophie sweated out all day by wearing a mask to raise money for Oxfam. She even wore it through games and everyone thought she was MAD!!

We raised £207 to help Oxfam make it a fairer world. Leap day has gone but that is no reason not to save our world by keeping our paper and putting it in a paper-bank. You can also test your cans to see if they are aluminium and you could ask your teacher if you could have a box or tray to put all the paper in that has been used in class and when it is full put it in a paper-bank.

We had fun finding out and learning about how to make it a fairer world for us and all living things. YOU CAN ENJOY IT TOO!!

*Nicki Dennes* (9)
*Sophie Allum* (10)

When you get some change at a shop put it in the charity box.

*Daniel Robinson*

Write letters to industry asking them not to dump so much waste.

*anon.*

We could look after any old people near us and do their shopping for them. We could also try to collect cans or whatever *Blue Peter* is collecting. People should give money to different charities. We could have a Bring and Buy sale with some friends. We could also write letters to our MPs and ask them to try and help all the poor and starving people. Not take things for granted. If we could change places with an Ethiopian child for one day we would never complain about small things again.

*Gillian Eva   (10)*

In our school we have 'a bowl of rice day'. We pay for our lunches but only eat a bowl of rice. The money saved is then sent to help the poor to live a better life.

*anon.*

We could have jumble sales and sell toys, books, games and clothes and send the money to Oxfam. They send the money to people who want to help themselves. If we listen to the people in the poor countries we know what they need. If they have no water we can work with them to make wells and send them what they need – these things we can buy with the money we get from our jumble sale.

*anon.*

Each supermarket should have a special bin to collect one particular item which would be of value to someone in need e.g. jumpers, spectacle frames, tins of food etc.

*anon.*

I WOULD LIKE TO SEE MORE PEOPLE WRITING TO THEIR M.P's ABOUT ANY INJUSTICE THEY SEE

*anon.*

### Raising Money for a Fairer World

Hold a 'Find the Frog' competition. Draw a big pond with twenty-four squares in it (but you can make a lot more squares if you want). Then get a piece of tracing-paper the same size as the pond, and draw a frog on it. Make sure the frog is inside one of the squares of your pond. Then charge people five pence (or more) a go to try and guess which square the frog is in. You write their names in the squares on the pond, or you can number each square and give people a piece of paper for them to write down the number of their square, and their name.

Whoever guessed the square the frog is in wins the game, and you can get quite a lot of money for Oxfam.

*Heather Coates*

*Luke*   (5)

We did a concert and a puppet show and made
and sold jam sandwiches to people who came.

*Sarah Gray*
*Rachel Gibson*

When I heard what was going on in parts of
Africa I decided that I had to do something and
raise some money for you . . . We had a disco and
charged people 50p to come in. Twenty-one
people came. We gave them biscuits and cake.
My baby brother came, but we only charged him
three pence.

*Eleanor Perry*

I dressed up and pushed someone three and a
half miles in a wheelchair. We were both
sponsored for this.

*Kirsty Andrew*

I did a sponsored slide in my local park. I went
down the slide 131 times in one hour and I raised
£8.50.

*Melanie Briggs*

Me and my three friends (Debbie, Fay and Alex)
are going to go vegetarian for two weeks and get
sponsored. I'm starting on 9 March because it's
my birthday on 3 March and I might want a
sausage that day.

*Beth Greenslade*

I'm getting sponsored to do as many jumps on horseback as I can in one minute. There are three of us doing this so it'll last for three minutes. Sorry it can't be longer but we have to think of the horses (and our bums).

If the ground is too hard or too soft, leave the horses in the stable and do the jumping yourself – that's what we'll do!

*Wendy and Pegg (the horse)*

We're doing a sponsored stay-awake. Me and my friends will stay awake for a whole twenty-four hours. We'll get lots of people to sponsor us – I've already got forty-one.

*Chetra Singh*

I'm a volunteer in a shop. I'm the youngest volunteer but I've been there the longest. I'm not at all ashamed of working in a charity shop.

*J Lumsden*

We're doing rubbish collection – going round all the houses and taking all their rubbish away to the skip, and charging people for it.

*Rebecca Cahill*

My mum and I are going to play Scrabble for twenty-four hours and get people to sponsor us. We both shop at Oxfam.

*Caroline Knaggs*

I can help to make the world fairer by washing cars, doing the washing-up, hoovering etc. Then I can send the money to Oxfam.

*Nicola Sylvester-Thorne*

Raise money doing a gymnastics show.

*Jessica Langford*   (7)

Here are some ways to make a fairer world. We could have a sponsored silence and a book sale or hold a clothes sale. We could also give up sweets for a month. So we can save money for the poor. We can also have a twelve hour fast.

*Claire* (5)

Dear Sir/Madam

I'm very sorry for all the people who are starving. I am in the Girls Brigade and my two leaders told us we were to collect pennies in Smartie tubes to give to Oxfam. We took all the pennies to an Oxfam shop in Lerwick (in Shetland) and we had collected about thirty pounds. It wasn't much but I was glad I did a small bit for Oxfam and I want to help as much as I can.

*Love from*
*Margaret Birnie* (10)

## A Question Game

**INSTRUCTIONS**

Players: 2 or more
What you need: 1 dice
Do what the squares tell you!
Maybe if you land on an action square you can help to tidy the world in some way.

*Amelia Ewart* (11)

START

TRY AND CLEAN UP THE RUBBISH YOU SEE ON THE GROUND

TRY AND USE EVERY THING YOU can AGAIN

Go FOWARD 2 SPACES.

Go BACK 3 SPACES.

Use areadoy And things like that Without CFC's

Be KIND to People

Take all your bottles + cans to the bottle bank + can bank.

Go forward 2 spaces

TRY to get Dolphin friendly sea food.

Use biodegradable bags

TRY AND make the WORLD A PLACE better to Live in.

FINISH

TRY AND HELP THE WORLD!

## Bookmark for a Fairer World

Why not make your own?

1.  Trace or copy the shape on the next page on to a thin piece of card. Mark where the holes for the butterfly fasteners are.
2.  Draw a person on the card with two speech bubbles, as on the picture.
3.  Trace or copy the shape of the arms and cut two out from thin card.
4.  Colour in your bookmark person.
5.  Attach the arms to the body with two butterfly paper fasteners.
6.  Use your bookmark everytime you read a book!

*Pupil from 1R St Teilo's School*

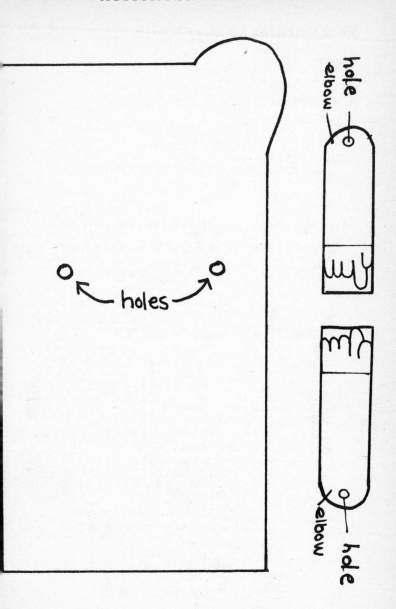

## Our World Cake

### Ingredients

½ teaspoon of health
1 teaspoon of love
5 g of happiness
2 g of Worldwide togetherness
2 pints of clean water
1 Dove

### Method

Mix together thoroughly and bake for 10 years.
When you have finished you will have a fairer
world.

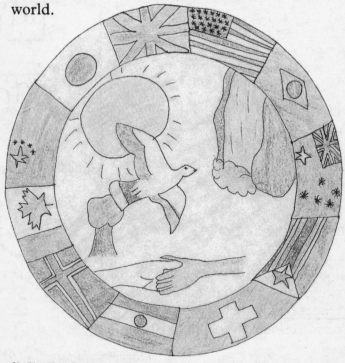

*Julie Bushell*  (11)

## A Fairer World Board Game

### HOW TO PLAY

Choose a counter and start at START.
Roll the dice.
The person who gets the highest number goes
first. If you land on a square with an *, miss a
turn. The person who arrives at FINISH first is
the winner.

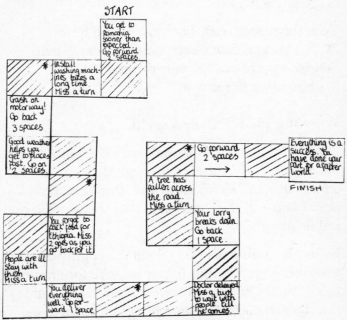

I chose to do a board game because it shows
people that they can take clothes and toys to
places that will take your things for poorer
countries like Romania or Ethiopia.

*Harriet Simpson*   (10)

# ABOUT OXFAM

*A Million Ways to a Fairer World* is a special book, because all the ideas in it have come from children and young people like you. OXFAM and Puffin set the challenge: to write in any way about what you would do, or could do, to make the world a fairer place. This book contains just some of the ideas that you came up with, of ways to help people help themselves.

You, the reader of this book, can join with OXFAM, which has been helping people help themselves around the world since 1942, in working for a fairer world.

## Working for a Fairer World

The main theme is 'fairness', with the phrase 'It's not fair that . . .' running through the contributions. We all know that there are many poor people in the world, and that the world is an unfair place.

Every day millions of people in the countries of the 'South' go without things we take for granted: food, shelter, water, education, health care, and the right to make decisions about our own lives. For many poor people things are getting worse, not better.

OXFAM is helping these people break out of their poverty by supporting them as they make changes that will last.

## The Early Years

In 1942 the world was at war. In Oxford, on
5 October 1942, a group a people formed the
Oxford Committee for Famine Relief. Its aim was
to help people in Greece, where women and
children were starving, and to campaign for food
and medicines to be allowed into Greece. It was
partly successful, and a trickle of food did get
through before the war ended.

When peace came in 1945 the Oxford Committee
found there When peace came in 1945 the Oxford
Committee found there was still work to do. It
raised money and collected clothing for refugees
in Europe. In 1948 it opened the first shop, in
Oxford, and in 1965 took the name OXFAM.

## OXFAM Overseas

OXFAM works in seventy-seven countries. A lot
of its work is in places where war and conflicts
make life almost unbearable for innocent victims.

OXFAM still carries out emergency relief. Maybe
you've seen the OXFAM Emergencies warehouse
on television, loading supplies for a disaster area.
But OXFAM also cares about the more lasting
relief of suffering, too. It works with very poor
people and helps them find ways to break free of
sickness, illiteracy and poverty. OXFAM helps
poor people question the unfairness that keeps
people poor.

OXFAM staff keep in regular contact with

projects abroad. Many self-help projects only need a little money to get started. About a third of OXFAM grants are for under £3,000, but these small sums can have a big impact.

Here are just three examples of OXFAM-funded work overseas, all working for a fairer world.

- In **Brazil**, working with children who have to live on the streets in the cities and towns of north-east Brazil, and supporting a popular education programme.
- In **Malawi**, helping to give shelter in refugee camps for over 700,000 people fleeing the conflict in Mozambique.
- In **Cambodia**, repairing much of the fresh water supply system in the capital, Phnom Penh.

If you want to know more about OXFAM-supported projects contact any of the addresses at the end of this section.

## OXFAM in the UK and Ireland

In 1942 the Oxford Committee campaigned to get aid to Greece. OXFAM still campaigns and tries to inform people and Governments about what can be done to help poor people tackle poverty and global injustice. *A Million Ways to a Fairer World* is a part of this work.

OXFAM also means shops. There are over 850 OXFAM shops in the United Kingdom and Ireland and you may have bought this book from one of them. The OXFAM catalogue is crammed with 'fair trade' goods made in projects overseas.

OXFAM started most of the fund-raising ideas that are common now: sponsored events; concerts; books (like this one); national Bring and Buy sales (started with *Blue Peter*), and many others.

Over the years OXFAM has become an international family of independent organisations spread across the world.

## OXFAM: Working for a Fairer World

Since 1942 OXFAM has given support to *people*, no matter what their race, colour, gender, politics or religion. This support can come in many ways:

- for a woman who can get safe drinking water from a new well in her village;
- as shelter for a refugee, even for a short time;
- through two meals a day, instead of one, as a result of improved agricultural methods;
- by someone being prepared to listen to your troubles;
- through the joy of a family whose child's life has been saved by simple medical care;
- by the lifting of some oppression through the action of unknown friends in a far-off country who care enough to lobby their MP and make their voices heard.

OXFAM provides an opportunity for everyone to make this support possible; to make our world a fairer place.

There are many ways you can help OXFAM work for a fairer world. You could:

- give good quality books, toys, clothes or other things you no longer need to an OXFAM shop;
- save stamps or coins and drop them off at an OXFAM shop;
- organize a social event (a party, jumble sale or Bring and Buy sale) to raise money for OXFAM;
- talk to other people about ways of working for a fairer world and get yourself and them involved.

Most of all you could refuse to give up on the world!

Thank you for buying *A Million Ways to a Fairer World*. You have already contributed to OXFAM's work as money from each copy sold supports OXFAM's literacy fund. We hope you will enjoy the book now you know something more about OXFAM and that we can count on your support in the future WORKING FOR A FAIRER WORLD.

To find out more about OXFAM write to us:

in **England**: OXFAM Anniversary Information, 274 Banbury Road, Oxford OX2 7DZ

in **Ireland**: OXFAM, 202 Lower Rathmines Road, Dublin 6

in **Northern Ireland**: OXFAM, PO Box 70, 52–54 Dublin Road, Belfast BT2 7HN

in **Scotland**: OXFAM, Fleming House, Floor 5, 134 Renfrew Street, Glasgow G3 3T

in **Wales**: OXFAM, 46–48 Station Road, Llanishen, Cardiff CF4 5LU

in **Australia**: Community Aid Abroad, 156 George Street, Fitzroy, Victoria 3065

in **Belgium**: OXFAM Belgique, 39 Rue de Conseil, 1050 Bruxelles

in **Canada**: OXFAM Canada, 251 Laurier Avenue W, Room 301, Ottawa, Ontario K1P 5J6

in **Hong Kong**: OXFAM, Ground Floor – 3B, June Garden, 28 Tung Chau Street, Tai Kok Tsui, Kowloon, Hong Kong

in **New Zealand**: OXFAM New Zealand, Room 101 La Gonda House, 203 Karangahape Road, Auckland 1

in **Quebec**: OXFAM Quebec, 169 Rue St Paul est, Montreal 127, Quebec H2Y 1G8

in the **USA**: OXFAM America, 115 Broadway, Boston, Massachusetts 02116

# CONTRIBUTIONS FROM

Anderson's Primary School, Forres, Scotland
Anglophone Section, International Primary School,
    France
Attleborough High School, Norwich
Aysgarth School, Bedale, N Yorks
Baston School, Bromley, Kent
Bishopwood School, Tring, Herts
Brune Park School, Hampshire
Canovee National School, Carrigadrohid, Co. Cork,
    Ireland
Carlton-le-Willows School, Nottingham
Clover Hill County First School, Norwich
Coaltown of Wemyss Primary School, Fife, Scotland
Codnor C E Junior School, Derby
Coxmoor Primary School, Sutton-in-Ashfield, Notts
Crossroads Primary School, Banchory,
    Kincardineshire
Darfield J & I School, Barnsley, Yorks
Downham Market High School, Norfolk
Exton C E Primary School, Rutland, Leicestershire
Fernwood Junior School, Nottingham
High March School, Beaconsfield, Bucks
High School of Dundee, Dundee
Histon Junior School, Histon, Cambs
Holy Trinity C E Primary School, Burnley, Lancs
Hook Lane School, Welling, Kent
The International School of the Algarve, Portugal
Kimberworth Comprehensive School, Rotherham
Krozno Odrzanskie High School, Krozno Odrzanskie,
    Poland

Le Verseau International School, Belgium
Lenamore Primary School, Galliagh, Derry,
   N Ireland
Letterfrack N.S., Co. Galway, Ireland
Lettergesh National School, Co. Galway, Ireland
Liskeard Infants' School, Cornwall
Longhill School, Brighton, East Sussex
Maypole House School, Alford, Lincs
Nanzan International School, Japan
New Haw County Middle, Weybridge, Surrey
North Combined First Middle School, Southall,
   Middlesex
North Roe Primary School, Shetland Islands
Our Lady of the Sea Primary School, Liverpool
Peel Clothworkers School, Isle of Man
Ras Al Khaimah English Speaking School, UAE
Runnymede College, Madrid, Spain
St Andrew's School, Salisbury, Wiltshire
St Christopher's School, Farnham, Surrey
St Christopher's School, Wembley Park, Middlesex
St Francis de Sales Convent, Tring, Herts
St John the Baptist, Kingston-on-Thames
St Joseph's Prep School, Reading, Berks
St Monan's Primary School, Fife, Scotland
St Paul's Walden School, Hitchin, Herts
Stanford Middle School, Surrey
Stoke St Michael County Primary School, Bath
Toucan Primary School
Upland Infant School, Bexleyheath, Kent
Wilshere Dacre C P School, Hitchin, Herts

And thanks to all the schools who sent in their 'Bricks
   to a Fairer World Poster' including:

Alexander Dickson Primary School, Bally Gowan,
   N Ireland

Alloa Academy, Stirling, Scotland
Annermoor Primary School, Tamworth, Staffs
Arthur Dye Primary School, Cheltenham,
  Gloucestershire
Battle and Langton C E School, Battle, East Sussex
Bemrose Community School, Derby
Brookfields School, Tilehurst, Reading, Berks
Cranston Primary School, Pathhead, Midlothian
The Crescent School, Oxford
Dame Catherine's School, Derby
Duagh School, Co. Kerry, Ireland
Dulwich College, London
Eastfield Primary School, Penicuik, Midlothian
Edgehill College, Bideford, North Devon
Ednam School, Kelso, Roxburghshire
Eureka Secondary School, Kells, Co. Meath, Ireland
F. C. J. Primary School, St Saviour, Jersey, Channel
  Islands
Gascoigne Junior School, Barking, Essex
Gringer Hill School, Maidenhead, Berks
Grovelands First School, Walton-on-Thames, Surrey
Haroldswick Primary School, Unst, Shetland
Heycroft Primary School, Leigh-on-Sea, Essex
Higham on the Hill Primary School, Nuneaton,
  Warks
Hillcrest School, Birmingham
Houndsfield Primary School, London
Hudson County Primary School, Liverpool
International School of London, London
Junior High School, Shetland
Kingsmead School, Wirral, Lancs
Leicester Islamic Academy, Leicester
Longacre School, Shamley Green, Surrey
Madam Lau Kam Lung Secondary School, Hong
  Kong

Millbrook Primary School, Grove, Wantage, Oxon
Nether Green Middle School, Sheffield
North Ealing Combined School, London
Oakfield School, Barnsley, Yorks
Oakland County Infant School, Wilmslow, Cheshire
Presentation Convent, Co. Cork, Ireland
Primrose Hill C P School, Chorley, Lancs
Roseburn Primary School, Edinburgh
Roughwood Junior School, Rotherham, Yorkshire
South Holderness School, Preston, Hull
St Barnabas' C E Primary School, Tunbridge Wells,
    Kent
St John the Baptist C E Primary School, Waltham
    Chase, Hampshire
St Joseph's Boys School, Co. Monaghan, Ireland
St Joseph's Primary School, Crayford, Kent
St Joseph's R C School, Penarth, South Glamorgan
St Mary's Middle School, Oxted, Surrey
St Teilo's C W High School, Penylan, Cardiff
Stanford Middle School, Norbury, London
Stanway County Primary School, Colchester
Swinton Primary School, Glasgow
Talbot Primary School, Leeds
The Queen's School, Kew, Surrey
Werrington Junior and Infant School, Yeolmbridge,
    Launceston, Cornwall

# USEFUL ORGANIZATIONS

Friends of the Earth
26–28 Underwood Street
London
N1 7JQ

Greenpeace
30–31 Islington Green
London
N1 8XE

Royal Society for the Protection of Birds
The Lodge
Sandy
Bedfordshire
SG19 2DL

The Tidy Britain Group
The Pier
Wigan
WN3 4EX

Population Concern
231 Tottenham Court Road
London
W1P 9AE

The Aluminium Can Recycling Association
1-Mex House
52 Butcher Street
Birmingham
B1 1QY

Beauty Without Cruelty
37 Avebury Avenue
Tonbridge
Kent
TN9 1TL

Royal Society for the Prevention of Cruelty to Animals
The Causeway
Horsham
West Sussex
RH12 1HG

Traidcraft (for Third World Products)
Kingsway
Gateshead
Newcastle upon Tyne
NE11 0NE

Intermediate Technology Development Group
Myson House
Railway Terrace
Rugby
Warwickshire
CV21 3HT

Animal Aid
7 Castle Street
Tonbridge
Kent
TW9 1BH

Henry Doubleday Research Association
National Centre for Organic Gardening
Ryton Gardens
Ryton-on-Dunsmore
Coventry
CV8 3LG

# ANSWERS TO PUZZLES

**CRACK THE CODE**

Chad
Ethiopia
Sudan

**ENVIRONMENTAL WORDSEARCH**

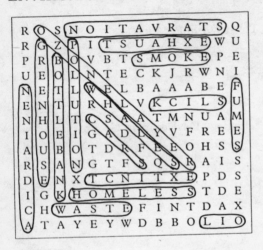

**WHICH LINE?**

Line B

# CROSSWORD FOR A FAIRER WORLD

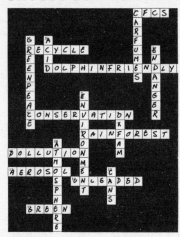

# RIDDLE-ME-REES

Bicycle
World

# WORLD WORDSEARCH

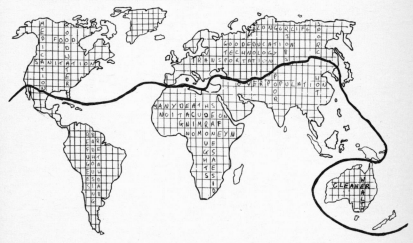

*Some other Puffins*

## THE CRACK-A-JOKE BOOK
*Chosen by children in aid of OXFAM*

This revised edition of *The Crack-a-Joke Book* is even more special than the original because it is a way of saying 'happy 50th birthday' to Oxfam. It still has all the best of the old jokes – but there's a new section of specially collected jokes for Oxfam's 50th anniversary too!

## THE PUFFIN SUMMER FUN BOOK
*Rose Griffiths*

What will you do today? You could try making alligators or zig-zag books, elephant sandwiches or skeletons. You could try playing crazy golf or have a treasure hunt. There are quiet things to do, and not so quiet things to do; things to do on your own or things to do with a friend. In fact, here's an A–Z of activities that will keep you going after school, at weekends and during the holidays, all the year round!

## ENVIRONMENTALLY YOURS
*Early Times*

What is the greenhouse effect? Why is the earth getting warmer? Who is responsible for the destruction of the countryside? Where can you get advice on recycling? When will the earth's resources run out? The answers to all these questions and many more are given in this forthright and informative book. Topics such as transport, industry, agriculture, population and energy are covered as well as lists of 'green' organizations and useful addresses.

## ANIMAL KIND
*Early Times*

*Animal Kind* looks at what humans are doing to animals. It also looks at what humans *could* be doing for animals to make their lives happier and to lessen their suffering. This is a hard-hitting book that covers topics such as vivisection, vegetarianism, farming, wildlife, pets and blood sports. It will help you look again at your relationship to the animal world.

# THE ALIENS ARE COMING

*Phil Gates*

The greenhouse effect is warming up the earth so that snowmen could become an endangered species. It also means you may have to eat more ice-cream to keep cool in summer. But worse, it may cause the spread of alien plants which will cause havoc in the countryside and could cause some native plants, which like a cool moist climate, to become extinct.

Find out for yourself, through the experiments and information in this original and entertaining book, just what is happening now and what is likely to happen in the future.

Become a scientist and help warn the world about the dangers ahead!

# LAND AHOY! THE STORY OF CHRISTOPHER COLUMBUS

*Scoular Anderson*

The colour of the sea was probably the last thing that Christopher Columbus was thinking about when he set off, five hundred years ago, on one of the greatest voyages of discovery ever made. His journey was just as adventurous and just as important as the first space flight to the moon was this century. But Columbus set sail into the vast ocean not really knowing where he was going or, once he had got there, what he'd found!

Now you can be an explorer by reading this book and finding out just what an extraordinary man Columbus was – how he managed to travel the world and put America on the map for the first time.